© Aladdin Books Ltd 2001

Designed and produced by
Aladdin Books Ltd
28 Percy Street
London W1P 0LD

*First published in
the United States in 2001 by*
Copper Beech Books,
an imprint of
The Millbrook Press
2 Old New Milford Road
Brookfield, Connecticut 06804

ISBN 0-7613-2174-8

*Cataloging-in-Publication data is on
file at the Library of Congress*

Printed in Belgium
All rights reserved

Coordinator
Jim Pipe

Design
Flick, Book Design and Graphics

Picture Research
Brian Hunter Smart

My World

My Home

By Tammy J. Schlepp

Copper Beech Books
Brookfield, Connecticut

2

Hi, I'm Rosa. My home is in the city. Look how tall my building is!

My apartment is way up high. We use the elevator to get home.

taking the elevator

Other people in our building live above us and below us.

My sister Beth and I share a room. We have bunk beds.

bunk beds

I get the top bunk. At night, I love to look out at the city lights.

city lights

City people hurry here and there.
I like to watch them from the bus.

Taxi cabs go zoom, zoom, zoom!
Drivers honk their horns to say,
"Get out of my way!"

bus

city street

The city is
the best
place to be!

Hi, I'm Jack.

My home is in the country.

Our house is in the middle of fields and meadows.

I play hide and seek in the bushes in our yard.

My Dad has a workshop. We are building a birdhouse. He cuts the wood with a saw.

hammer

nails

I rub the wood with sandpaper to make it smooth.

Then we use a hammer and nails to put the birdhouse together.

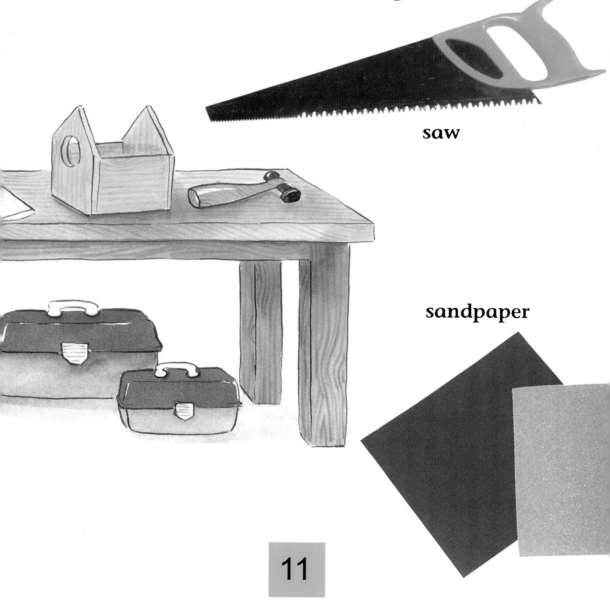

saw

sandpaper

The Jacksons are our neighbors.
They live on a farm.

They have cows, chickens,
and pigs.

Sometimes Mr. Jackson lets
me sit on his tractor.

The country is the best
place to be!

tractor

Hi, I'm Nicky.

I live in a town
between the city
and the country.

Towns like mine are
called suburbs.

Houses on my street have
lawns and trees and bushes.

Our house has three floors.

My room is at the top in the attic.

attic room

I have to climb up the stairs to get to my room.

sliding down
the banister

But I don't have to go down the stairs. I can slide down!

My friends Joe and Billy
live next door.

We swing on a rope in
Billy's yard.

rope swing

We ride our bicycles up and down the sidewalk.

riding bicycles

The suburbs are the best place to be!

Rosa, Jack, and Nicky live
in different places.

Where do you live?

What do you like
about your home?

Here are some words and phrases from the book.

swing on a rope

ride on a bus

sleep in bunk beds

in the country

sit on a tractor

slide down the banister

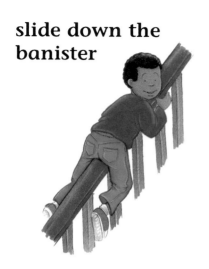

live in the city

elevator

ride bicycles

Can you use these words to write your own story?

Did you see these in the book?

poster

scooter

clouds

carpet

Illustrator: Mary Lonsdale for SGA

Picture Credits:
Abbreviations : t–top, m–middle, b–bottom, r–right, l–left, c–center.
2, 5, 23tr–Corbis. 7, 9, 10 both, 11 both, 12, 14-15, 16, 24
all–Select Pictures. 18, 22tl–Digital Stock.